OFFICE
PASTIMES

50 THINGS
TO DO IN **THE OFFICE**
THAT WON'T GET YOU A P45

MARCUS WEEKS

OFFICE
PASTIMES

Ivy Press

First published in 2006 by
Ivy Press
The Old Candlemakers
West Street, Lewes
East Sussex BN7 2NZ, UK
www.ivy-group.co.uk

ISBN 10 1-905695-12-8
ISBN 13 978-1-905695-12-6

Ivy Press
This book was conceived, designed,
and produced by Ivy Press.

Creative Director: PETER BRIDGEWATER
Publisher: JASON HOOK
Editorial Director: CAROLINE EARLE
Art Director: SARAH HOWERD
Designer: JANE LANAWAY
Illustrator: JOHN WOODCOCK
Photography: SIMON PUNTER
Pastime Practitioner: ANNA DAVIES

BRITISH LIBRARY CATALOGUING-IN-PUBLICATION DATA AVAILABLE

Printed in Thailand
3 4 5 6 7 8 9 10

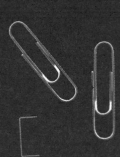

Contents

 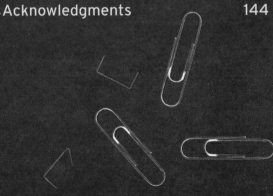

Introduction

As technology progresses by leaps and bounds, more of the dirty, dangerous, and tedious work is done by machines. The number of blue-collar workers is decreasing exponentially as production becomes more labor efficient. The curious thing is that, at the same time, the mind-blowing advances in computer technology have created *more* work for the administrative side of businesses. A hundred years ago, a factory might have had 95 percent of its workforce involved in production, administered by the remaining 5 percent of office staff; nowadays, the situation is totally reversed. In fact, the process has gone so far that many companies are now 100 percent office workers.

And now that all of the nitty-gritty is done by machines, instead of having more leisure time, we're all working longer hours in offices, managing ever more complex administrative systems in companies producing less and less. It can all becomes a little demoralizing if you think about it too much, so it's better just to call it an expanding service-industry sector and move on.

The trouble is that the sort of work that we end up doing much of the time can be dull and repetitive, and job satisfaction more often comes from clawing your way up the office hierarchy than from doing any productive work. Some companies have realized that if they want to prevent their staff from leaving in droves, and to make sure that they actually do some work while they are at their desks, it's a good idea to provide them with leisure facilities (a bit like hanging a mirror in a parrot's cage). So big corporations now offer their employees gyms, saunas, and social clubs.

But what if you work in a company that can't afford those incentives? Yup, that's right: that's where this book comes in handy. Here are fifty ways to make your day at work a more joyful experience and to keep you working at your optimum efficiency level. Well, maybe that's going a little too far, but at least the projects in this small volume will help you have more fun and will give you an added incentive to show up at work every day.

You won't need any expertise or previous experience to enjoy these pastimes, nor will you require any special equipment other than what you can find in just about any office. So give them a try. Discover your creative side, build up some team spirit, and be a bit adventurous. Pretty soon, you'll actually be looking forward to arriving at work!

WARNING | While the majority of these activities can be attempted safely, this book is intended only as a humorous reference source. No responsibility can be taken by the publishers or the author for any loss, injury, or damage occasioned by reliance on the information contained herein. Care should always be taken to ensure that no permanent damage is done to office property, and pastimes requiring physical exertion should not be attempted by anyone with health problems. If in doubt, seek professional advice.

1

OFFICE CRAFTS

For most regular people, working in an office not only is brain-achingly tedious but also lacks the satisfaction of seeing an end product. Even the humblest operative on an assembly line can point with pride at a nut, screw, or sprocket and say, "I made that," but it's difficult to feel the same sense of creative achievement when looking at a well-kept file cabinet or a neatly presented report. Let's face it, all that most of us produce is yet more work, and we're more likely to come away from a meeting thinking about the really neat doodle that we've just drawn than about the establishment of a fourth subcommittee.

But it doesn't need to be like that, of course. Instead of sitting there, blankly staring out the window, playing your 454,356th game of solitaire, or accessing all of those dubious Web sites e-mailed to you by your colleagues, you could use your downtime to satisfy those creative urges. All it takes is a little practice and a bit of imagination to transform the raw materials found in every office into decorative and useful crafts, at the same time fulfilling the artistic inner you.

13

Bulldog-clip Zoo

- BULLDOG CLIPS
  (in a variety of sizes)
- BINDER CLIPS
- CORRECTION FLUID
- PAPER CLIPS
- COFFEE STIRRERS
  (optional)
- MOUNTING PUTTY

One of the main beefs about office life is its distance from the tooth and claw of life in the wild. Change all that by creating your own zoo—or at least a pet store—of animals assembled from that supply-room mainstay, the bulldog clip. We made a diplodocus here, but feel free to experiment.

1| Your basic building blocks are standard bulldog clips. Vary the sizes so that you can get the scale of your animal right. Include different styles of bulldog clips for flexibility of design.

TIP|*Lay out your bulldog clips in the intended animal shape. Trace the outline before you begin.*

2| The basic assembly maneuver is to open the first bulldog clip and snap it onto one of the ring-pull handles of the second. You can then lay down both bulldog clips as shown. Repeat as necessary.

ADVANCED WORK|

Create enclosures for your animals using white plastic coffee stirrers and blobs of mounting putty. Set close together, these make convincing white picket fences.

3| To make the body and neck curve, affix bulldog clips to one another at an angle. Use smaller bulldog clips for the neck, and binder clips for the face and tail. Dab on correction-fluid eyes if you like.

TIP|*Start small in order to perfect your clipping technique. This mouse is simply constructed from three bulldog clips and a customized paper clip.*

Ballpoint Architecture

YOU WILL NEED

- BALLPOINT PENS *(lots)*
- TRANSPARENT TAPE
- MOUSE PAD
- CARDBOARD
- PAPER CLIPS
- MOUNTING PUTTY

From the pyramids of ancient Egypt, through the Classical temples of Greece, to the Empire State Building, some of the greatest and most enduring monuments to human creativity have been architectural. Now, in your own small way, you, too, can achieve a degree of immortality right there at your desk, by erecting miniature wonders of the world, follies, or simple dwellings, using humble writing implements and office equipment as your construction materials. OK, they may not last as long as Machu Picchu, but then Rome wasn't built in a day . . .

TIP | *Remember that a ballpoint pen has three component parts: the outer tube (or case), the inner tube (the actual pen), and the cap. The outer tube is the basic building block; the flexible, inner tube is useful for joints and corners; and the cap can be used for decoration or as roofing material.*

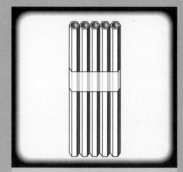

1| Disassemble all of your ballpoint pens and line up the outer cases. Make walls by fixing rows of cases together with tape on both sides.

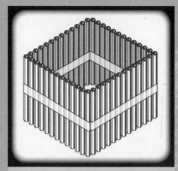

2| Stand the outer wall upright on a mouse pad. Build up the inner walls to the required height using cardboard to support the layers. Use straightened paper clips or pen tubes to brace corners.

3| Construct a roof spire by taping together an elegant arrangement of complete pens.

4| Position the spire and apply pen caps around the base of the roof with mounting putty as decoration.

Pencil Fort and Stockade

YOU WILL NEED

- MOUSE PAD OR CLIPBOARD
- PENCILS *(lots)*
- NAIL FILE OR PENKNIFE
- MOUNTING PUTTY
- PAPER CLIPS

If you've had enough of urban cityscapes and yearn for the ruggedness of the wild, wild West, a fort may be more your thing. Since this project uses more traditional building techniques, you might like to substitute pencils for ballpoint pens to create a rustic effect.

TIP | *Once you've successfully mastered the techniques of ballpoint and pencil building, you can branch out and extend your architectural skills. Designing your own dream house can be fun; just remember that the materials lend themselves best to Modernist style (ballpoint pens) or Backwoods Rustic style (pencils).*

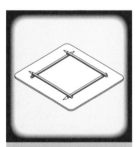

1 | Mark out the foundations on a clipboard or mouse pad and lay out the platform.

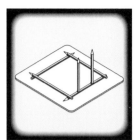

2| Cut two pencils in half. Erect a doorway by fixing the pencils upright with mounting putty. Trim down more pencils to create walls on either side.

3| Build up the pencil walls using mounting putty to hold the layers in place. Reinforce corners with bent paper clips.

4| Putty an outer wall of sharpened uprights to form a stockade around your fort. Now prepare to defend it against attack.

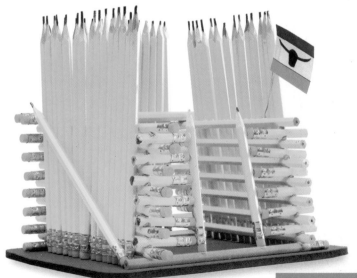

Hole-punch Snow Globe

YOU WILL NEED

- HOLE PUNCH
- PLASTIC FOLDERS OR DIVIDERS
- SMALL GLASS JAR WITH A SCREW-TOP LID
- COMPANY MAGAZINE *(optional)*
- GLUE
- MOUNTING PUTTY
- PERMANENT MARKER

Few of life's frivolous objects are more cheering than a snow globe, and it is easier to make your own than you may think. Snow globes make effective stress busters (shake one when you're feeling extra tense) and powerful office mojoes (give one a couple of vigorous turns before that interview, and promotion will be yours). Stick with traditional yuletide scenes and white snow, or customize your creations to make personalized gifts for your colleagues.

Suggestions...

Why not re-create your own office building in a snow globe? Leave it on the CEO's desk, and you could end up as the production manager of the promotional gifts department.

1| Make the snowflakes by punching holes in plastic folders or dividers. (Paper will dissolve.) Colored flakes make for jazzier snow globes.

2| Clean out a glass screw-top jar. (You could borrow one from either the office cafeteria or the nerd who brings in his own relish for sandwiches.)

3| Create a snow-globe background. Either draw your own or cut one out from the company magazine. Glue it to the outside of the jar, with the image facing inward.

4| Make small models and figures out of mounting putty. Define their features with a permanent marker. Arrange them and then stick them firmly to the inside of the lid.

5| Add the snowflakes to the jar. Add cold water, pouring it in slowly. Screw the lid on *tightly*, then turn the jar upside down to allow any excess water to drain away. Now shake your snow globe.

TIP|*For a really professional finish, add a few drops of glycerol to the water. This will result in better suspension.*

ADVANCED TIP|*If your figures look too low down, give them a boost by gluing a thick disk of polystyrene (the packaging that comes with electronic equipment is a good source of this) inside the lid. Use opened staples to skewer your putty creations securely to the polystyrene disk.*

Supply-closet Jewelry

Here's an idea that will not only keep you occupied during your coffee breaks but will get you noticed, too. Look in the supply closet, and you should find everything that you need to make some seriously eye-catching jewelry, either for yourself or as a truly personal gift. You can choose between the flashy bling of the paper clips and thumbtacks or the ethnic chunkiness of the erasers and pen tops, but whatever you make, it's bound to be unique, and will be the talk of the office party.

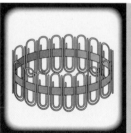

Rubber-band bracelet Choose a wide rubber band (or use two together) that will fit your wrist comfortably. Decorate it by clipping paper clips all the way around, either side by side for a simple bracelet or overlapping for a chunky bangle. Why not hang trinkets off these to make a novel charm bracelet?

TIP *Let your imagination run free: all sorts of hitherto unnoticed objects from around the office can be threaded onto string, clipped onto rubber bands, or stuck onto cardboard to make jazzy baubles, bangles, and bling. And don't forget that you can add a touch of color by using permanent markers.*

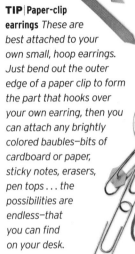

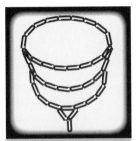

Paper-clip necklace This can be as simple or as elaborate as you like. The basic chain is made by linking together paper clips to the required length; you can then hang further decorative paper-clip chains from that. Use different-sized paper clips for different effects.

Eraser pendant Push a straightened-out paper clip through one end of an eraser and bend it to form a loop; this can then be hung from a paper-clip chain. A row of different-sized erasers makes a dramatic necklace.

TIP | Paper-clip earrings *These are best attached to your own small, hoop earrings. Just bend out the outer edge of a paper clip to form the part that hooks over your own earring, then you can attach any brightly colored baubles—bits of cardboard or paper, sticky notes, erasers, pen tops . . . the possibilities are endless—that you can find on your desk.*

Thumbtack punk-style choker Cut a 1-inch-wide strip of thin cardboard long enough to go around your neck plus a couple of inches. Color it black with a permanent marker. Stick a row of thumbtacks on it with mounting putty, and then fix them permanently in place with a strip of transparent tape and (optional) decorate the edges with staples. Cut slits halfway through at either end to make a clasp, and wear it with Goth-style makeup and attitude.

23

Awareness Raising

Remember the craze for wearing wristbands or ribbons that told the world which good cause you supported? They were a type of fashion statement with a message, and so much cooler than a badge. In return for a donation, you got to wear your heart on your sleeve. Well, if you've got a campaign or slogan you'd like to publicize around the office ("Make filing history," or "Make love, not layoffs," maybe), it's easy to make bands and ribbons to sell or give to supportive colleagues.

YOU WILL NEED

- FELT-TIP MARKERS
- LARGE, WIDE RUBBER BANDS
- COLORED PAPER
- TRANSPARENT TAPE
- SCISSORS
- PINS

WRISTBANDS

Wristbands are really simple to make. Using a felt-tip marker, write your slogan (in capital letters) on a wide rubber band. Just remember to use rubber bands that are both big enough for regular people to wear without cutting off the blood supply to their hands and wide enough to write your slogan legibly. For more discreet messages, replace words with meaningful symbols.

RIBBONS

Take a piece of colored paper and stick a length of transparent tape along one edge. Turn the paper over and repeat on the other side. Now cut this tape-covered strip from the sheet and then divide it into lengths of about 4 inches. These can then be curled into the appropriate shape before being stapled together and pinned to clothes. (Alternatively, you may find some ribbon lying around the office somewhere . . .)

TIP *Be very careful about the campaign, and especially the slogan, that you choose. Open defiance of company policy is seldom a good idea, and some issues can provoke extreme reactions. The ribbons are a safer option for controversial campaigns, since it is often only the wearers who know what they're all about.*

Eraser-henge

Offices are, generally speaking, not the most spiritual places in the world, and they are more temples to mammon than to any deity. They're also usually found in cities, miles away from any sign of nature. But there is a way of creating a little New Age corner for yourself so that you can get away from the hustle and bustle and commune with the spirit of Mother Earth without leaving your desk. It's easy to make a replica of England's Stonehenge with just a few erasers, after which the druidical rituals and pagan rites that you can perform are limited only by your imagination.

1 | Mark out the circle of your henge on a mouse pad or clipboard, and decide where to place the central altar.

2 | Arrange upright erasers around this circle, using mounting putty if you need greater stability.

TIP | *You may think that your eraser-henge looks, well, a bit too perfect. That's because we're used to seeing really old henges that have been knocked about over the centuries. To age your eraser-henge, distress the individual "stones" with a nail file, and judiciously knock down, or even remove, a couple of them.*

3 | Lay horizontal erasers on top of the uprights.

4 | Stack two or three erasers in the center to form an altar, and then align the whole henge to catch the sun at dawn on Midsummer Day.

Cafeteria Construction

One of the downsides of working behind a computer monitor is the lack of outlets for physical energy. Don't you sometimes long to swagger around in a hard hat, effortlessly swinging a sledgehammer? If you work for a corporation that provides an in-house cafeteria, there is a way to express your inner engineer: buy two meals—one to eat, and one to reconstruct—and then use your fork and some spoons for the heavy spadework and toothpicks for the fine detailing.

CARROT-HENGE

Here is a simple carrot-henge on a druidical base of garden peas to show how basic post-and-beam and monolithic construction works. Once you have mastered this, you can adapt it to suit more modern buildings. It is particularly suitable for the Chicago Skyscraper style.

MOUNT FUJI

Start with natural forms, because these are more forgiving of structural mistakes. Shown here is Mount Fuji (ideal if you work for a Japanese-owned consortium). Establish a bedrock of cauliflower or broccoli florets before mounding up the mashed potatoes. We used cottage cheese for the snow, but you can achieve a similar effect with yogurt or sour cream. Don't be afraid to use dessert building materials to create stunning effects.

TIP | *Why not work with colleagues to produce entire hometowns, cityscapes, or mountain ranges?*

THE SYCOPHANT'S OPTION

Re-create your own office building. Sign it in ketchup. Make sure that you leave your tray outside the directors' dining room where your boss can see it.

TIP | *When constructing any high-rise edifice, first spread out a layer of mashed potatoes in which to sink the foundation piles securely.*

Office Installation

YOU WILL NEED

- LIMITLESS IMAGINATION
- WHATEVER YOU CAN FIND IN THE OFFICE

Art isn't what it used to be. It's no longer necessary to have a particular skill, such as drawing, painting, or carving. No, nowadays it's all conceptual, which means that the concept is more important than the finished object (I think). And now that artists don't have to make a painting or sculpture but can *create* an installation, it leaves the field wide open to do whatever you think may be a good idea, arranging whatever you have on hand in a way that you think looks good. It's as simple as that (I think).

Collect all of the mice from the computers in the office and arrange them around your lunchtime cheeseburger.

Get some brown paper and string from the supply closet and wrap your computer, chair, and desk in it.

Make as much mess as you can on and around your work space, and then invite people to come and look at it.

The minimalist option is to clear your desktop completely, clean it, and then sign your name in very small letters in one corner.

WARNING | *Don't be too upset if your efforts aren't immediately appreciated by your colleagues. It's possible that you're just too avant-garde for them. It's particularly galling if the office cleaners tidy up or throw out your work overnight, but don't let this deter you: all of the great artists have had to put up with philistines.*

TIP | *To preserve your masterpieces for posterity, take pictures of them on your cell phone. You can then send these to friends and colleagues who may not be able to come into the office to see your art.*

Staple-block Tumble Game

A little handicraft is needed to make the building blocks for this classic game, but you'll be ready to play in next to no time if you follow the simple instructions. Set up the blocks and then invite your colleagues to join you in a match—how could they resist the challenge? It's a deceptively simple game that demands extremes of skill and strategy, and also nerves of steel as you take risks that could end in disaster.

WARNING|*Beware of cheats with magnets.*

TIP|*Once you've built a set of staple bricks, they can be used again and again, so why not organize a tumble-game league in the office? Your games will soon become a spectator sport, too, and somebody's bound to start taking bets. This could be just the thing to improve office morale and build team spirit.*

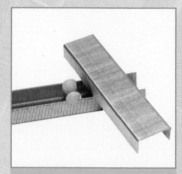

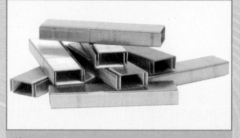

2| To prepare the game Stack your staple bricks in rows of three to the required height.

1| To make the bricks Staples come joined together in long blocks, and these can easily be snapped into pieces of the appropriate length (between 1 and 2 inches, depending on the size of the staples). Join two of these together with a little mounting putty or glue (see the illustration), and you have the basic brick for your game. Make sure that all of the bricks are of the same size, and ideally use fairly large staples.

3| To play the game Take turns to remove one brick at a time from the bottom or middle of the stack and put it on the top. The first player to knock over the stack loses. The trick is to make the stack as unstable as possible for your opponent, without making it too difficult for yourself.

WARNING *This game may not be suitable for use in earthquake zones, nor for those of a nervous disposition.*

Coffee-break Cootie-catcher

YOU WILL NEED

- A SQUARE PIECE OF PAPER
- COLORED PENS

There's always a heated debate about whose turn it is to make the coffee, who should go out and buy the cookies, and who didn't wash out their cup. Now you can put an end to all of this discontent by consulting the coffee-break cootie-catcher, which is just like the ones that you made as a kid, but customized to solve the most frequent disputes around the office coffee machine. You can make it even more fun by adding a couple of dares or fortunes, too. Remember, the cootie-catcher's decision is final!

MAKING A COOTIE-CATCHER

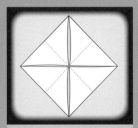

1 | Take a square sheet of paper and fold each corner point into the center.

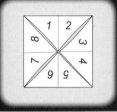

2 | Flip it over and fold the four corner points into the center again. Write the numbers 1-8 on the triangles (see diagram).

HOW TO PLAY THE COFFEE-BREAK COOTIE-CATCHER GAME

1| Ask one of your colleagues to choose a color from the four on the top flaps of your cootie-catcher.

2| Spell out the color chosen, moving the flaps in and out with your fingers in time as you pronounce the letters.

3| Open the cootie-catcher to show four of the eight numbers and ask your colleague to choose one; now count up to this number in the same manner.

4| Ask your colleague to pick another number from the four now revealed and count again; then ask him or her to choose one of the numbers finally displayed. Open the appropriate flap and read out the "fortune."

Suggested "Fortunes"

You could include the following "fortunes" and messages:
➜ it's your turn to make the coffee
➜ we all know your guilty secret
➜ you have an admirer in the accounts department
➜ the previous player will be your slave for the day
➜ you have to make the coffee for the rest of the week
➜ ask your boss for a raise

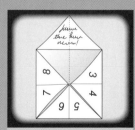

3| Lift each flap and write a fortune or dare underneath.

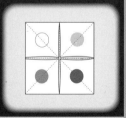

4| Flip it over and color or write the name of a color on each flap.

5| Flip over again and stick your two thumbs and two forefingers into each of the four flap pockets to work the cootie-catcher.

2

OFF(ICE) BROADWAY

Even the most introverted office worker secretly longs for the razzmatazz of the world of showbiz. The lure of the bright lights, the siren call of the adoring crowds . . . who wouldn't give up their humdrum office job for all of that, given half a chance? Although it's unlikely that you'll ever be in a position to give up the day job, you can, however, have a taste of the high life by organizing some imaginative amateur dramatics to perform in your office.

There's probably a wealth of talent lurking behind those desks, just waiting to be discovered—not only actors and musicians, but scriptwriters, lighting engineers, set designers, and so on—and you could be the executive producer who pulls it all together. You could think big and produce a full-scale Broadway musical, you could create a more modest puppet theater, or you may find that your company is more suited to a historical art-house production or a TV-style drama.

Whatever you decide on, you'll find that there really is no business like show business, and that office business may have to take a backseat at times. But the show must go on, so get out there and break a leg!

Office! The Musical

While working in your office every day, you may have overlooked the fact that it is the ideal setting for a Broadway-style musical. All of the elements are there: a cast of dozens of very different characters, intrigues and rivalries, secret passions and unrequited lusts, triumphs and disasters. And the set—what could be better than all of that floor space, with desks and chairs to dance on and with, and all of the props that you could wish for? All that you have to do is write the script, cast the stars, and organize the rehearsals . . .

Some suggestions to get you going . . .

Don't worry if your script seems contrived and banal, the story unbelievable, and the songs completely unnecessary to the plot. That's not a failing on your part—it's how most musicals are. As long as you perform your musical with huge confidence and sincerity, nobody will notice.

THE SHOW

Although it would be great to write a completely original script, with new songs and dance routines, it may be safer to start out by adapting one of the classics to your office environment. How about *Desk Side Story, The Phantom of the Office, A Chorus Line Manager,* or *Porgy and Best Practice in the Workplace?* You get the idea? That way you can use the basic story line and put in the office characters while using the tunes as vehicles for your own words.

AUDITIONS

Organize auditions during coffee and lunch breaks, and be realistic about the abilities of your coworkers. If they don't have what it takes, it's better to relegate them to the chorus from the beginning than to have to pull in an understudy for the first night—that would be a cliché

OPENING NIGHT

After months of rehearsals, you'll be ready for the show. A classic way to start is for you to leap spontaneously from your seat (note that spontaneity takes a lot of practice) and shout out to the entire department, "Hey everybody, why don't we do the show right here?" It then only remains for you all to run through the agonies and ecstasies of your chosen musical and to finish with the members of the entire cast giving it their all in the grand finale.

PARTY TIME

The opening-night party is, of course, mandatory, as it gives everyone the opportunity to congratulate one another and then bitch behind their backs for the rest of the evening.

TIP *There's no need for elaborate sets (unless you really want them), since the musical is set in the office, and the same goes for costumes (although people do love dressing up). Lighting shouldn't be a problem either, with all of those desk lamps and strip lights. I leave makeup to your discretion.*

41

Office Soap Opera

- GOOD IMPROVISATIONAL SKILLS

- A VIVID IMAGINATION

Nobody will ever admit to being addicted to a TV drama, but it's strange how everyone knows what's going on in the plot of each and every one of them. But there's no need to be ashamed of your encyclopedic knowledge of its goings-on if you're the creator of the drama. Office workers are forever being asked to take part in role-playing exercises as part of their in-house training, so they'll all jump at the chance when you ask them to perform in their own office soap opera, and the whole thing will practically write itself from then on.

Some suggestions to get you going . . .

Ask everyone in the office to submit story lines and suggest the characters that they would like to play. Come up with a really good title (something like *Six Feet Under Paperwork*, *Twin Geeks*, *I Love Loose Leaves*—I'm sure that you'll think of something). Have a brainstorming session to figure out who's going to be who and to come up with a few starting points for drama-filled plot lines.

Suggested Plot Lines

Here are a couple of suggestions to get you thinking soap.

TROUBLE AT CONFECTIONERY GIANT SWEETY PIES

Ambitious Penny Whistle is appointed new marketing director, to the dismay of salesman Tom Sellitt, who is disappointed. He seeks his revenge by threatening to reveal her murky past in dental research. Meanwhile, the tragic accident in the elevator has exposed the love affair between CEO Charlie "Pop" Sickle and his pretty young secretary, and has caused the miraculous return of the memory of the deaf janitor . . .

ALL CHANGE AT INVISIBLE INC.

Since the move to luxurious new premises, life has been tough for the Invisible staff. The investigation into the murder of Finance Director Ivor Scampland continues, and officer Cy Kopath is interviewing suspects and uncovering more than he bargained for. The murky tale of money-laundering goes right to the top, implicating Seymour Bux, the company founder in a sleazy deal fronted by his marketing director, Les Scruples . . .

TIP|*When there is a real drama in the workplace, such as a takeover of the company, an unexpected promotion, or a mysterious pregnancy, this could be incorporated into the plot of the soap opera. In fact, if a cast member left the company, it would have to be.*

continued on page 44

Office Soap Opera

Here's an episode of office soap *DESPERATE COWORKERS* to inspire you. It's just an everyday story of life, love, schemes, and scandal . . . and it's going on in an office somewhere, right now.

TIP | *Allocate fifteen minutes every day to the office soap opera, when everyone should act in character, and let the story develop as it will.*

TIP | *Once a week—on Friday afternoons, say—have a recap ("Previously, on Desperate Coworkers . . . "). Try to end each episode on a cliff-hanger, especially just before the weekend.*

Britney tells Jolene about her affair with babe-magnet Irving from Finance. Jolene knows Irving is the biggest philanderer in the building.

Bob hurries to the boss's office to tell him everything he knows.

Britney surprises a couple in an intimate embrace in the supply room. It is none other than philandering Irving and slutty gold-digger Mandy.

Meanwhile . . . Jim has been researching Tim 's suspect sales records and tells Bob just how Tim has been getting so many orders lately.

But . . . The boss doesn't want to hear Bob's news! Tim is his secret love child and is already blackmailing him. He fires Bob on the spot!

Next time on *Desperate Coworkers* . . .

Will Bob get his revenge? Is the boss's secret safe? Will Britney use her pregnancy to trap Irving? Tune in next time to find out!

Brown-bag Theater

Just over the wall of your cubicle, there is a colleague sitting, eating lunch, who is just as bored as you are. Perhaps a little matinee performance would cheer both of you up. It only takes a couple of minutes to make puppets out of bags, and then it's on with the show! A Punch-and-Judy show would be an obvious choice to brighten up the lunch break, but you don't have to restrict yourself: you could perform your own versions of popular TV shows or a few impressions of your boss and some of the office eccentrics.

TIP|*Start simply, with a children's puppet-style show, before going upscale and trying your hand at Japanese Noh theater, Greek tragedy, and so on.*

1 | Eat your lunch.

2 | Clean all traces of mayo, butter, oil, and so on from the bag.

3 | Draw a face on the bag with a felt-tip marker.

TIP | *When you've mastered the genre, you can become even more ambitious and try scaling down some of the big epics, such as* Star Wars *or* Ben Hur.

4 | Steal other people's lunch bags (and their lunch, if you're hungry) and repeat the process, making different characters with different facial expressions.

5 | Insert your hands into the bags and, using these as hand puppets, perform the show over your cubicle wall.

Paper-cup Puppetry

YOU
WILL
NEED

- PAPER CUPS *(different sizes if you can find them)*
- TRANSPARENT TAPE
- STRING
- BURGER BOXES
- FELT-TIP MARKERS
- TWO RULERS

At some stage, nearly every kid invents an imaginary friend, not just to have someone to talk to but to have someone to blame, and someone who'll say what the kid really thinks without worrying about the consequences. Wouldn't it be neat to have someone like that as an adult? Someone you could take along to meetings who would say it like it is, and take the flak, too? Well, meet Mr. Dick C. Beaker, your imaginary friend made real, and your constant companion and confidant. Take him to your meetings, and he'll dare to say the things that you only thought . . .

48

WARNING| You'll have to learn a bit of ventriloquism to get Mr. Beaker to voice your opinions, but as everybody will be watching him, not you, you won't have to be that good. Remember: if you want him to be taken seriously, you'll have to play it dead serious.

1| Collect paper cups and tape them together in pairs as shown, and then thread string through them to form arms and legs that are jointed at the elbows and knees.

2| Cut more cups to form hands, and add them to the arms. Similarly, add flattened cups to make feet.

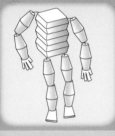

3| Tape together burger boxes to make a body, and then tie on the arms and legs.

4| Make a head from a burger box, draw on a face, and then join it to the body with a string neck.

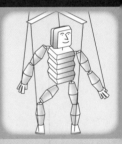

5| Attach strings to the top of the head, wrists, and ankles, and the other ends of the string to a cross made from two rulers taped together.

Workplace Reenactments

There are, apparently, people who spend their weekends reenacting famous scenes from history and refighting decisive battles. They maintain that this gives them an insight into the issues and some idea of how it felt to be alive at the time, but I suspect that it's really just an excuse to dress up in some neat costumes and get rid of some pent-up aggression. Whatever the motivation, it may prove popular in your office, too. While a full-scale Waterloo may not be a practical idea, there are plenty of other historical moments that you may have loved to have been in the thick of.

TIP | *If history's not really your thing, you could choose some decisive moments in your company's past to re-create: the chaos of the stockroom fire of 1973, the chairman's retirement party in 1964, or the coffee famine of 1999, for example. Apart from anything else, there will probably be someone around who has first-hand knowledge of the occasion.*

Suggested Scenes

Here are a few ideas to get you started, but the possibilities are really only limited by your imagination.

THE ALAMO

This could be constructed from a desk and chairs, and the characters could be recognized by their distinctive hats.

SIGNING THE DECLARATION OF INDEPENDENCE

A simple tableau to set up, as long as someone can find a suitable feather to make into a quill pen.

THE FIRST MOON LANDING

Costumes could be a problem (although plastic wrap and aluminum foil could work), but the main fun will be from doing everything in slow motion.

COLUMBUS DISCOVERS THE NEW WORLD

Columbus steps ashore from his workstation and greets the natives.

Office Orchestra

A great way to instill team spirit in any workforce is to get them all making music together. That's how brass bands, male-voice choirs, and even some orchestras started out, as a leisure activity to keep the workers happy. Unfortunately, it's not that easy anymore, and the cost of musical instruments and equipment is prohibitive—unless, of course, you make your own. OK, the sound quality may not be up to professional standards, but the pride that your musicians will take in playing instruments that they have made themselves will more than make up for that.

COMB-AND-PAPER KAZOOS
Wrap a comb in a sheet of thin, stiff paper. (Tracing paper is ideal, as is hard toilet paper, but you can't find that anymore. Progress? Hah!) Press to your lips and hum. The kazoo should vibrate and buzz in sympathy.

GLASS GLOCKENSPIEL
(GLASSES AND BOTTLES)

Put as many glasses and bottles as you can find on your desk and see which give out the highest and lowest notes when tapped with a pen or pencil. Line them up, ranging from the lowest-sounding one on the left to the highest on the right. To alter the pitch of any of them—especially if there are several that produce about the same note—experiment with different levels of water in each one in turn.

WARNING *The glass glockenspiel is not only the trickiest instrument to make but also the hardest to play effectively, so perhaps it should be given to someone who has some musical expertise. Other instruments can be safely entrusted to complete musical beginners without spoiling the overall effect too much.*

MAILING-TUBE DIDGERIDOOS

Take a long mailing tube (or the inside tube from a roll of paper) and apply one end to your mouth. Now blow hard through your closed lips, making them vibrate in a vulgar manner; the effect at the other end of the tube should be quite melodious. For a deeper note, tape two tubes together end to end.

Office Orchestra

Having made your melody instruments (the comb-and-paper kazoos to carry the main tune, the glass glockenspiel for all of the fussy parts, and the mailing-tube didgeridoos to provide a drone), it only remains to get yourselves a rhythm section . . .

RUBBER-BAND GUITAR

Well, more of a harp really, but you'd never get anyone to play that. Find a cardboard box (ideally about the size of a shoe box) and remove the lid. Stretch rubber bands of various sizes around the box and pluck them where they are stretched over the open side. If any of the "strings" are too loose, try shortening the rubber band by tying a knot in it on the opposite side of the box.

String bass | Trap one end of a piece of string in the drawer of a desk or file cabinet. Pull tight and pluck. Instant Charlie Mingus.

DRUM KIT

Using pen or pencil drumsticks, tap out rhythms on drums made from overturned trash cans, paper cups, and lunch boxes; cymbals made from desk-lamp shades; and cowbells made from cups and saucers.

TIP | *Don't forget to record your performances for posterity. You could either use the old-fashioned Dictaphones in the office closet or lay down a few tracks on the computer. You might like to try a live broadcast, too, either relayed via cell phones or, using the computer's internal mike, uploaded onto the Internet.*

DESKTOP LATIN AMERICAN SECTION

The various surfaces of your desk can be coaxed into producing a wealth of different sounds, from a low conga to a high bongo, by striking them with your fingertips, palms, and wrists, and scraping them with pens and pencils. To add to the fun, shake boxes and metallic containers that are half-full of paper clips, thumbtacks, and so on.

Coordinated Casual Fridays

It seems that most offices are encouraging informality these days, at least on one day of the week. To get away from the dull uniformity of suits and neckties or formal twin sets, workers are encouraged to dress down, brightening up the workplace with the individuality of blue jeans, sweatshirts, and sneakers. But why stop there? Why not encourage people to dress up rather than down? Each week there could be a different theme and a specified dress code, so that people would have to think carefully about what they wore instead of just putting on the first thing that came to mind. Now, wouldn't that make life more interesting?

TIP | *Give plenty of notice of what this week's theme is going to be so that everybody has a chance to make/ borrow/rent/steal a costume. Post details on the bulletin board or circulate them by internal e-mail.*

WARNING | *If yours is the kind of office that frequently has visitors or customers, it would be good to warn them about your dress-down policy. It could be very unnerving to arrive at a company staffed entirely by Laurel and Hardy look-alikes. But then they might also want to join in . . .*

Suggested Themes

Here are some themes
to get you started.

ELVIS DAY
Everybody does an Elvis
impersonation.

THE 1960S
Provides the opportunity to wear
wigs, as well as outrageous
clothes and makeup.

COPS AND ROBBERS
Come as your favorite TV
detective or villain.

DANCING FEET
Fred Astaire and Ginger Rogers.

WILD WEST
John Wayne, Clint Eastwood,
or *Little House on the Prairie*.

U.S. PRESIDENTS
From Washington to Bush.

SANTA CLAUS
Wouldn't it be great if everyone
came as Santa, especially in July?

CROSS-DRESSING
This one is likely to provoke
a very mixed reaction.

Ring-tone Jam Session

YOU WILL NEED

- A CELL PHONE EACH
- A MINIDIRECTORY OF EVERYONE'S NUMBERS

Cell phones are normally frowned upon in concert halls, but they are capable of such neat sounds these days that it would be a shame not to feature them somehow. Unlike traditional musical instruments, they require little—or no—skill to play, so it should be no problem getting a good-sized combo together to get on down for a really hot jam session. Not all of the cats in the pad will dig what's going down, but hey, that's cool, as long as it's got swing. And if you gotta ask what that is, you don't got it, baby.

TIP | *The interesting thing about playing a cell phone is that you're actually playing someone else's phone, so until it rings, you can't be sure how it's going to sound. What's more, you can stop the phone ringing by hanging up, but then so can its owner, by answering it. Weird.*

1 | At the downbeat from the musical director (MD), someone dials the number of his or her neighbor's cell phone. When this starts ringing, the jam is under way.

2 | Once the first ring tone has set up a steady groove, the MD can cue another player to dial. Once the next cell phone starts ringing, the session begins to get really interesting.

3| As the mood takes them, players can drop out or join in with the jam, and the mood will change subtly as they do so.

4| The complex counterpoint of the multiple cell phones can be punctuated by the shrill percussiveness of the landline ring tone, too, making an interesting contrast.

ADVANCED TIP|

Although some ring tones are recognizable melodies, it's best to have cell phones set to play more abstract sounds and rhythmic patterns, perhaps with just one well-known tune sounding over the top once a groove has been set up.

5| If possible, give everyone the chance to perform a solo, then work up to a storming climax with all phones blaring, and watch the MD for the cue to bring everything to a close to the accompaniment of wild applause.

3

CUBICLE FUN

Whether you work in one of those open-plan offices where everybody can see what everybody else is up to, or one of the more modern places where you're stuck in your own little cubicle, your workspace can be a mighty dull and lonely place. But there's no need just to sit there and put up with it—oh, no. You can start making changes right now that will transform your personal space into the haven that you're cravin' and organize ways of communicating with your coworkers that will not only bring the workforce together but will also provide endless entertainment.

Why not start by giving your cubicle a thorough makeover—not just putting up a few photos of the spouse and kids, but making it really your own? Or even doing the same for a colleague? And when you have things how you'd like them, you'll want to invite the neighbors around to take a look, so you'll have to find a way of contacting them that's a little bit more—how shall I put it?—*adventurous* than just popping around or sending an e-mail. And once communications have been established, the fun and games can really get going . . .

63

Paper-cup Telephone

YOU WILL NEED

- PAPER CUPS
- A SHARP PEN OR PENCIL
- STRING
- FRIENDS

OK, so the guy at the next desk is within shouting distance, and you could easily lean over to chew the fat with him, but this way's much more fun. Just a little preparation, and you'll have your own personal internal telephone system, a dedicated line for person-to-person calls without the risk of others eavesdropping. Once the system's up and running, you'll find that you have to use phrases like "over," "roger," and "over and out," just like for CB radio, so why not go the whole hog and invent your own call signs and silly names, like Rubber Deskie or Big Business?

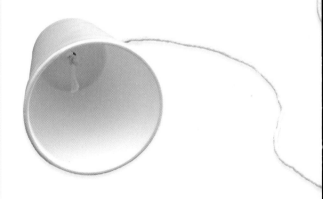

1 | Make small holes in the bottoms of two paper cups (using a very sharp pen or pencil should do the trick).

2 | Thread some string through the hole inside one cup and make a knot to prevent it from being pulled through.

3 | Measure out enough of the string to reach the person with whom you wish to talk, cut it to this length, and then repeat step 2 with the second cup.

TIP | *Each person must grip his or her cup quite firmly, because it is essential that the string is taut if proper communication is to be established. It's also best if the string doesn't touch anything else, so try to avoid it going around corners.*

4 | Pull the string tight and talk into one cup while the other person listens through the other cup.

5 | A three-way (or four-way, or maybe even more—try it!) conference call can be made by connecting multiple cups to a central hub with string—but be warned that keeping all of the strings tight will be tricky.

Feng Shui

YOU WILL NEED

• A GOOD SENSE OF DIRECTION

Go on, admit it: your desk's a mess, the wall's covered in sticky notes dating back years, and you can never find anything. Not exactly the best conditions for efficient working, eh? So what are you going to do about it? Undertake the annual blitz that just makes matters worse because you end up throwing away the important stuff and keeping all of the useless trash? Or will you take a tip or two from the ancient wisdom of the Orient and organize your workspace to promote calm, success, and well-being? The choice is yours, but I know what I'd do . . .

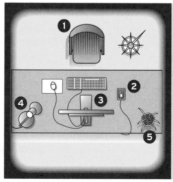

1| Apply feng shui to your desk and get rid of all inauspicious artifacts. (NB: Ensure that there are no mountains in front of you.)

1 High-backed chair
2 Telephone
3 Computer
4 Lamp
5 Flowers

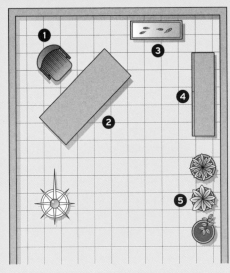

1 High-backed chair
2 Desk
3 Aquarium
4 Cupboards (not open shelves)
5 Plants

2| Arrange the furniture in auspicious positions around your cubicle. (NB: Ensure that your workspace is not directly beside, or beneath, a bathroom. This is most inauspicious.)

3| Ensure you are seated facing the most beneficial direction. Hang up a wind chime and use red ribbons in place of binder clips.

TIP| *Wear the right colors to get you noticed by the boss, or to promote a sense of well-being, as follows:*
➲ *green for confidence and growth*
➲ *red, yellow, or orange for yang energy, giving strength, recognition, and respect*
➲ *black and blue to calm tempers and curb enthusiasm*
➲ *white for authority*

TIP| *Remember: never send red flowers to your boss. If you really must send some, choose yellow ones.*

WARNING| *Once you start using the principles of feng shui, it's very easy to become carried away. Although you may think that it's a good idea to introduce a fountain or mountain into the office, not everybody will agree, and making all of the cubicles face the right way may not be practical either.*

I Spy

With all of the closed-circuit television cameras around at the moment, and the degree of paranoia that exists in most offices, you could be forgiven for thinking that Big Brother is watching your every move. But if you want a slice of the surveillance action, too, you could make a neat lo-tech periscope with stuff that you can find in any office. Then you will be able to keep an eye on the goings-on in adjacent cubicles using an unobtrusive spying device that didn't cost a fortune. You could also use it when you're up to something that you shouldn't be and need to keep a lookout for the manager coming around.

1| Get ahold of a few of those big, fat mailing tubes from the mail room, and cut them into two lengths of about 6 inches and one length of about 2 feet.

TIP *CDs work pretty well as mirrors, but to be honest, the resolution isn't all that great. If you can lay your hands on a couple of real mirrors instead (try raiding a few makeup bags, or carry out some excavation work in the executive bathroom), it will make all the difference.*

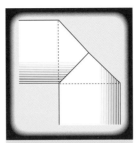

2| Cut one end of each 6-inch tube and both ends of the long tube at angles as illustrated. Glue or tape them together.

3| Take a couple of unwanted CDs and glue them across the diagonal holes at each corner (with the shiny side facing inward), ensuring that they don't let in any light (you'll probably have to cover the hole in the middle with a piece of cardboard).

Online Consequences

This is a hi-tech version of an old Victorian parlor game, updated for modern office use. The original involved writing phrases on a piece of paper and then folding down the top and passing it to the next player, who couldn't see what had been written before. But in the new, "paperless" office (ha!), there's now a much more efficient way of playing consequences. Each player makes a contribution to the story as it goes along, unaware of the other players' ideas, and a suitably surreal result is assured. And the consequences of all of this? A happy workforce, and another hour or so satisfactorily wasted.

Suggested Categories

Use your imagination to add extra ones:

- ⮑ adjective(s)
- ⮑ boy's name
- ⮑ adjective(s)
- ⮑ girl's name
- ⮑ a place
- ⮑ he gave her
- ⮑ he said

TIP | *This is a game for any number of players, but because it's a bit complicated, it may be better to start off with just two until you get the hang of it.*

This is a bit tricky, so concentrate . . . and remember, the important thing is that nobody should see what the others have written until the very end of the game.

1| Set up an e-mail account called "Consequences," or something similar.

2| Player 1 now thinks of an adjective that could describe a person, writes it in an e-mail, and sends it to the "Consequences" account (Subject: "1. Adjective"). Then he e-mails the next player, asking him or her to think of a boy's name.

3| Player 2 thinks of a boy's name and e-mails it to the "Consequences" account (Subject: "2. Boy's name") before e-mailing the next player asking for another adjective.

4| This player then sends his or her adjective to the "Consequences" account (Subject: "3. Adjective") and e-mails the next player, asking for a girl's name.

5| The process is continued in a similar vein, adding a place name, what he gave her, what he said, what she said, and then the consequences.

6| Gather around the computer on which the "Consequences" account was set up and open the e-mails one by one to see the story unfold.

Consequences
You'll end up with results like this:

- ⮑ [the] incredibly handsome
- ⮑ Henry Kissinger
- ⮑ [met]
- ⮑ cute and adorable
- ⮑ Queen Victoria
- ⮑ [at] Niagara Falls
- ⮑ [he gave her]
- ⮑ a large plastic bag
- ⮑ [and he said]
- ⮑ "I've always wanted to be able to tango"
- ⮑ [she said]
- ⮑ "Please be gentle with me"
- ⮑ [and the consequence was]
- ⮑ an earthquake in a remote South American village

WARNING|*Be careful who sees the finished games, for experience has shown that most players tend to include a few characters from inside the company, and you may fall foul of the libel laws if you enter the wrong name in the "Mail to" field.*

Office-jargon Bingo

Amazingly, bingo is still hugely popular, despite requiring as much skill as getting up in the morning, and being as interesting as watching a plank warp. The office version lifts this humdrum time-waster into the realms of the sublime, though, by combining the elements of satire and competition in a simple game format. Meetings that you used to dread, chaired by that idiot with the degree in management-speak, will become the high point of your week, and you'll be hanging on her every word. With a bit of luck, she'll never find out what has caused your sudden enthusiasm for her meaningless business babble.

TIP | *Encourage players to jot down any new words or phrases that they hear that don't yet appear on the bingo cards. These can then be included in a new set of cards for the next meeting.*

1 | Mark up a set of cards, one for each player, with a grid of nine boxes.

synergy	band-width	brick-2-clicks
e-tailing	outside the box	face time
put to bed	parachute someone in	water-cooler moment

2| Write a word or phrase of typical management jargon in each box (it doesn't matter if you duplicate one or two, but on different cards, of course).

3| Hand out the cards to the participants just before the meeting.

4| During the meeting, when one of the phrases in a box is used, the player crosses it off on his or her card.

5| The first player to cross off all of his or her boxes shouts "Office!" (as opposed to the traditional "Bingo!") and wins the game.

6| If there is no outright winner, get together after the meeting and compare cards to see who scored the most hits.

Whose Workstation Is This?

Celebrity homes are often featured in glossy magazines and have even spawned some TV spin-offs where panelists are invited to guess the inhabitant of a luxury villa, for example, by the style of the décor. A good clue to the inhabitant's identity in these quizzes is often the study, especially the desk, which makes it ideally adaptable in this way for office entertainment. Go on, make a celebrity out of one of your coworkers: broadcast photos of his or her office habitat for everyone to giggle at. But just so that they don't become too smug, remind them that they don't know who's next . . .

1| First, choose your victim. It's best if you select someone whose desk is in a particularly messy state, to increase the embarrassment factor.

2| Wait until he or she is away from the cubicle, then sneak in and take a few photos that show the dump in all its glory.

3| Send or e-mail the photos to all of your colleagues, with the message, "Whose workstation is this?"

4| Wait for the barrage of replies to come in and then select a winner.

5| Award a prize—perhaps a computer-cleaning kit, a dustpan-and-brush set, or maybe a copy of this book.

TIP|*Some people have built up quite a local reputation for slovenliness, and, indeed, may be so well known in their own department that their cubicle is instantly recognizable to close colleagues. So it's best if you use pictures of a desk in another department, or else send photos of your neighbor's desk to friends in a remote part of the building.*

Deck the Pods

Christmas comes but once a year, and what do you do about it in your office? Put up a straggly and tired fake Christmas tree and hang a few baubles from your swing-arm lamp? Oh, come on, get into the spirit of the holiday season and go all out to make your workspace a celebration of all things yuletide. And don't stop there: instead of just putting on a silly hat for the last day at work, wear the complete Kriss Kringle outfit and march around the office ringing your bell and spreading goodwill to all—they'll love you for it!

YOU WILL NEED

- COLORED PAPER AND CARDBOARD
- SCISSORS
- ADHESIVE
- PAPER CLIPS
- FELT-TIP MARKERS
- STRING
- MOUNTING PUTTY
- CORRECTION FLUID
- HOLE PUNCH

TIP | *Why restrict yourself to Christmas? There are all sorts of festivals and holidays that you could celebrate by giving your cubicles a new look:*

- ➲ *the Fourth of July (think stars and stripes)*
- ➲ *Halloween (lanterns and pumpkins)*
- ➲ *Thanksgiving (a real turkey)*
- ➲ *Hanukkah*
- ➲ *Diwali*
- ➲ *your birthday*

If you put your mind to it, you could celebrate a different theme just about every week.

Hanging decoration Cut out stars, angels, Christmas trees, reindeer, and so on and thread them onto string as an attractive hanging decoration, or else stick them on the wall as a frieze. Decorate surfaces with cardboard holly leaves, and make fake mistletoe from green paper and a couple of balls of white mounting putty (or second-hand chewing gum).

Paper chains Make paper chains by cutting strips of colored paper and gluing them to form links.

Paper-clip tinsel Link paper clips to make tinsel-like chains.

Snow Give the office windows a sprinkling of "snow" using correction fluid, and scatter hole-punch snowflakes (see *Hole-punch Snow Globe,* pages 20-21) over the floor.

Christmas mailbox Turn your trash can into an office mailbox for internal Christmas cards.

Desktop Yard Sale

YOU WILL NEED

- JUNK
- PRICE LABELS
- THE GIFT OF THE GAB

A by-product of decluttering your workspace is, if not exactly garbage, well, clutter. There'll be all sorts of junk that you haven't used for years but really can't bring yourself to throw away—you'd much rather it went to a good home, to somebody who would make good use of it. If only you could hold a yard sale . . . hang on, why not? Well, it would be a shame to see it go to waste, and there must be someone who really needs a—heck, I don't even know what that is, but it's a bargain and yours for a buck and a half.

TIP | *Be realistic about pricing: the object of the exercise is to get rid of stuff, not to make a fortune. Better to let that superfluous staple remover go cheap than still to have it on your desk at the end of the day.*

1| First, do a major cleanup of your workspace. Make a space where you can pile anything that you think has to go, and then sift through it for items that you know just won't sell (but you'd be surprised, so keep an open mind).

2| Now completely clear the top of your desk.

3| Arrange the items for sale on your desk, sticking price labels on as you work. Instead of money, colleagues could barter or pay in kind, perhaps offering pledges to do your shift, bring you your morning coffee and pastry, and so on. Remember, this is your store window, so try to make it look attractive.

4| Announce the sale around the office, and prepare for the bargain-hunters to arrive. Toward the end of the day, you could try slashing prices to sell the last few items.

TIP| *An alternative is to hold a departmental auction to offload all of that unwanted bric-a-brac. Pin an announcement to the bulletin board and publish an in-house catalog by e-mail. With luck, you'll soon find your useless junk going, going—gone!*

Swing-arm-lamp Morse Code

You must have seen those great World War II movies about the convoys sailing across the North Atlantic Ocean. To maintain radio silence so that they didn't give anything away to the deadly German U-boats, the Allied crews sent messages from one ship to another using really cool outsized flashlights with louvered blinds attached, called Aldis lamps. By sending a series of short and long flashes (called dots and dashes), vital information could be passed on in Morse code. Cool! You may not be at sea, but you've got a swing-arm lamp, so you can now warn your buddy of the imminent arrival of the office supervisor.

WARNING *It's not always possible to obtain a line of sight between you and the recipient of your messages, so an alternative is, using a pen, to tap out Morse-code communications on a lamp shade, cubicle wall, or whatever makes a sound that carries well across the hubbub of the office. If you knock on the radiator, however, you may find that you're broadcasting to the whole building.*

1| Make sure that you and the person to whom you're sending your message know Morse code (see the tables to the right).

2| Point your swing-arm lamp at the person with whom you want to communicate. That's easy if he or she is directly in front of your desk, but you may need to angle your lamp over the cubicle wall to communicate with your next-door neighbor.

3| Using the rocker switch at the base of the lamp, flash your message in Morse code (you may have to practice creating long and short flashes before you start sending messages for real).

4| Give your colleague time to decode your message and set up his or her own lamp, and prepare to jot down the reply.

5| Take down the message and decode it.

6| Repeat as necessary.

THE ALPHABET IN MORSE CODE

Dash=long signal
Dot=short signal

A	•—
B	—•••
C	—•—•
D	—••
E	•
F	••—•
G	——•
H	••••
I	••
J	•———
K	—•—
L	•—••
M	——
N	—•
O	———
P	•——•
Q	——•—
R	•—•
S	•••
T	—
U	••—
V	•••—
W	•——
X	—••—
Y	—•——
Z	——••

NUMBERS IN MORSE CODE

The numbers one through nine, as well as zero, are transmitted in Morse code as follows:

1	•————
2	••———
3	•••——
4	••••—
5	•••••
6	—••••
7	——•••
8	———••
9	————•
0	—————

PUNCTUATION IN MORSE CODE

You can also punctuate in Morse code, as follows:

Punctuation	Code
.	•—•—•—
,	——••——
:	———•••
?	••——••
'	•————•
-	—••••—
/	—••—• or —•———•—
" "	•—••—•

State of Mind

YOU WILL NEED

- A MAP
  (for reference only)
- SCISSORS
- PAPER AND CARDBOARD
  (various colors)
- CORRECTION FLUID
- MIRRORS OR CDS
- TRANSPARENT TAPE
- STAPLES
- PAPER CLIPS
- DUCT TAPE
- STRING

It's all very well tidying up your workstation and getting rid of all of the garbage that's accumulated on your desk, but it ends up looking kind of empty. And because you've thrown away all of the executive toys and stuff, there's nothing to do, either. The perfect solution to both problems is to "terraform" the desktop. You can make a pretty neat relief map in staggeringly realistic three dimensions out of odds and ends from around the office, and in the process create a stunning aerial view of your home state, or even your own fantasy island.

TIP|*Invite colleagues to take a guided tour of your home state. You could point out places of particular historic significance (your birthplace, where you crashed your first automobile, and so on), as well as areas of outstanding natural beauty. You could even create a short son et lumière using your desk lamp.*

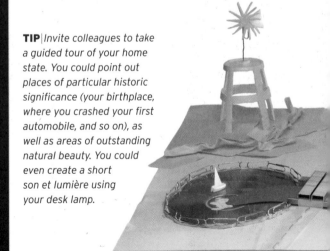

1 | Referring to a map of your state, cut out an outline of the area that you're going to re-create from a large sheet of paper. Use this as your base and lay it on the desk.

2 | Build up the underlying topography of the area. Colored paper or cardboard can represent farmland, plains, or desert; crumpled paper makes good mountain ranges; and forests can be created from small pieces of green paper rolled into the required shapes.

3 | Now add rivers, lakes, and any other bodies of water. Don't try to be too realistic when creating the water for your maps, as it can become awfully messy. It's a good idea to use mirrors or CDs for the lakes, tape for the rivers, and blue paper for the ocean.

4 | Add the major cities and other landmarks. Buildings, bridges, and so on can be constructed from blocks of staples, while smaller landmarks can be created from paper clips.

5 | Next, put in the main roads. Duct tape is good for this, but because it is usually way too wide, it will have to be cut into thin strips.

6 | Lay down your railroads. Mark out the routes for the lines with string, and then staple it down at regular intervals.

Cubicle Makeover

Goodness only knows why, but do-it-yourself is second only to fishing in the league of popular hobbies and has spawned a whole slew of TV series. Perhaps the best of these is one in which couples agree to swap houses for a while, and then give their friends' place a thorough makeover. The results are invariably terrible and lead to amusing confrontations between the participants. There's no need for you to miss out on all of this fun just because you're stuck in the office, however. You could swap with a colleague and make over each other's cubes, or just go in while he's on vacation and prepare a lovely surprise for his return.

Some suggestions to get you going . . .

Find a colleague to swap with, and then have a good look around his or her cubicle. Sketch some ideas and decide on a theme, color scheme, and so on. Be bold! You could, for instance, opt for a modern minimalist look (easy), the down-home rural style (moderately difficult), or eighteenth-century Rococo (tricky). Well, who knows? Once you've done a few makeovers you may make a buck or two as an interior designer.

1| Raid the supply closet and the marketing department's stash for making exhibition stands for anything that could be useful (like paints, colored paper, and screens).

2| Roll up your sleeves and start decorating.

3| Add the finishing touches, such as some plants, pictures, decorations, and accessories.

85

Relocation, Relocation, Relocation

As an alternative to the classic cubicle makeover, if two of your coworkers are away at the same time, give them something to puzzle over when they get back: just swap the entire contents of their cubicles, positioning everything as closely as possible to the way that it was in its original location. This works best if the people work in different departments, and preferably on different floors. Watch their faces as they settle down to work again, then see how long it takes before they figure out where everything went.

WARNING | *An important part of all of these jolly japes is maintaining a prim and proper expression when denying any part in the prank. Note that it takes practice to do this without snickering.*

Follow these tips for a smooth move:

THE PLAN
Make detailed plans and notes of the layouts of both cubicles, as well as what's on the walls and where.

THE MOVE
Disconnect all electrical equipment in both cubicles. Move large pieces of furniture—like desks, file cabinets, and closets—first. If you're careful and can get help, this can be done without disturbing either the contents or what's on top.

THE FINE DETAIL
Relocate all small ornaments, plants, and other odds and ends. Take down all of the pictures and bulletin boards and then rehang them appropriately.

TIP | *A variation on this theme can be achieved over lunchtime if you can assemble a task force that can work quickly. Simply remove everything from your absent colleague's cubicle and set it all up in the executive bathroom, hallway, supply closet, or elsewhere.*

Sticky-note Pranks

YOU WILL NEED

- STICKY NOTES
  (millions of 'em)

Experts in the field of business technology would have us believe that the computer is the single most revolutionary item in the modern office. Well, they're wrong—the elegant simplicity of the humble sticky note beats all of that electronic wizardry hands down, as far as I'm concerned. Let's face it, it takes forever for you to tell your machines to remind you to do anything, and then there's usually some glitch that messes everything up. The user-friendly sticky note has far less to go wrong with it (besides the adhesive stuff becoming covered in lint and losing its stickiness). And you can also do sooooo much more with sticky notes . . .

WARNING | *Your office supervisor may become suspicious if you suddenly requisition industrial quantities of sticky notes, so build up a supply over the course of a few weeks.*

TIP | *If you don't trust the adhesive qualities of your sticky notes, reinforce them with a little transparent tape.*

STICKY-NOTE TREASURE HUNT

Write a clue referring to a place in the office on a sticky note and stick it on your neighbor's computer. This will lead him or her to another sticky note on which is written another clue, and so on. At the final destination, hide a little treasure (a doughnut, the key to the executive bathroom, or whatever).

STICKY-NOTE PLASTERING

Wait until someone's out of the office for the morning. Then go into his or her cubicle and cover every available surface with sticky notes bearing messages reading, "While you were away . . ." Apart from the confusion that this will cause, the visual effect will be really stunning.

STICKY-NOTE MOSAIC

Use different-sized and different-colored sticky notes to create a stunning mosaic on an office wall. Abstract designs are good, or you could try experimenting with the company logo.

SPURIOUS MESSAGES

Leave a message written on a sticky note on your friend's (or enemy's?) desk, telling her to call a certain number at 10 a.m. On the phone whose number it is, leave another sticky note (preferably one of those sappy pink novelty ones) on which you've written the message "How about a really hot date? I'll call at 10," before signing it with your friend's (or enemy's) initials. Then sit back and wait for the fireworks.

4

OFFICE ACTION

We're all well aware of the dangers of our modern, sedentary lifestyle, which are made worse by lounging around the office all day, and we're constantly being encouraged to get some kind of exercise. If your office doesn't have its own gym, it's hard to work up the enthusiasm to go out and find one, and even if it does, most of us really don't want to go there. Apart from memories of school and the unattractive aroma of smelly sneakers, the stuff that you have to do in these places is even duller than sitting at your desk.

The answer, of course, is to get involved in some competitive or team sport, but that means doing it after work, unless your company has zillions of dollars to spend on staff facilities. Now there's a growing trend for exercises and sports that you can actually do in the office, and you can even buy kits, books, and DVDs on office golf, desk basketball, and how to perform aerobics at your workstation. Far be it for us to pooh-pooh these noble efforts, but wouldn't it be more fun to work out new ways of working out in the office, especially if they can get people together? Here are a few totally new sports that have been designed with the typical office worker in mind, and that don't require any special equipment—not even a ball.

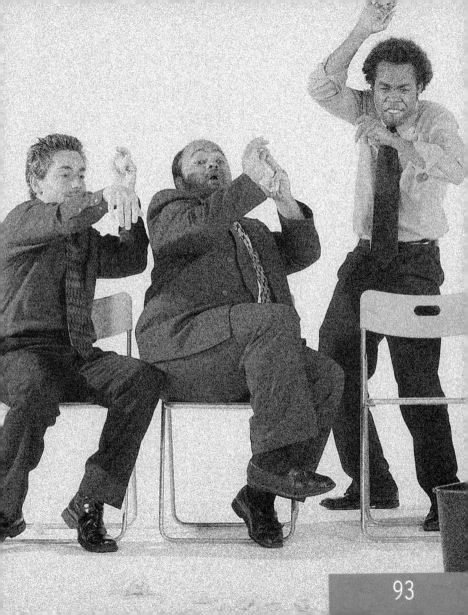

Synchronized Chair Spinning

When you eventually get around to organizing an office Olympics incorporating all of the games in this section, this would make a stunning spectacle for the opening ceremony: a team of athletes showing off their routines in perfect harmony. You may think that you'd need a lot of practice before being able to spin around elegantly and effortlessly on your office chair, but if you think about it, you've already learned all of the basic movements by twirling from the keyboard to the telephone, and then to the file cabinet, before scooting across the aisle to see your colleague. All that it takes now is a bit of time to figure out a display with your teammates—oh, and a suitable soundtrack.

WARNING

Make sure that all of the casters and swivel mechanisms are maintained and lubricated to their optimum performance. If necessary, order new office chairs, particularly if the old ones squeak.

Basic Steps

These are the basic steps for chair spinning.

LEFT TURN, RIGHT TURN

With one foot on the base of the chair, push around 90° (keep the other foot on the floor and use it as a brake).

BACKWARD

With both feet on the ground, push backward and freewheel.

FORWARD

With your heels on the ground, heave forward and freewheel.

SIDEWAYS

With one foot on the ground to one side of the chair, push; this can be combined with a 90° turn so that you either face the direction of movement or roll backward.

TIP | *Chair spinning can be performed as a competitive sport by dividing the office into teams and having a panel of judges award points for style, technical accomplishment, and so on.*

Advanced Steps

Once you've mastered the basics, it's time to learn the advanced steps.

PIROUETTE

As for the left turn, right turn, but give an almighty push with both feet, with your arms outstretched, before bringing them in to your sides as gracefully as you can.

HIGH KICKS

These are generally best done after pushing off for a backward run, when you push with one foot and raise the other leg high in the air as you freewheel backward.

ARM FLING

Throwing one arm, or both, violently to the side is a more spectacular way of starting a left or right turn, or even a pirouette.

Cube Ball

Racket games, such as tennis, squash, and badminton, normally require custom-made courts, but one of the beauties of modern offices (perhaps their only beauty) is that the walls between cubicles make an ideal "net" to play cube ball over. Cube ball is best played in a seated position on smooth-running office chairs; these give a great range of maneuverability, and skillful footwork can twist, turn, and glide an experienced player into the ideal spot for some of the trickier return shots. Once you've tried it, you'll be spoiled for the conventional games, and no longer will you have to admit, "I play good tennis, but badminton."

YOU WILL NEED

- WADDED-UP PAPER
- CLIPBOARDS

TIP | *Get a knockout competition going, or, better still, several: men's singles, ladies' singles, mixed doubles, and so on. Play for the coffee-cup trophy.*

TIP | *A simpler form of cube ball can be played without rackets, like volleyball. This is, perhaps, best played between teams of as many people as will comfortably fit into a cubicle.*

1| Make a ball from wadded-up paper.

2| Give clipboard bats to each player, and toss a coin to decide who serves first.

3| Player 1 serves the ball over the wall separating two cubicles.

4| Player 2 returns with a magnificent crosscourt volley.

5| Player 1 lobs the ball high over the cubicle wall.

6| Player 2 attempts a smash but fails to get the ball over the wall. It's fifteen: love. Player 1 serves again . . .

Chair Derby

The most exhilarating sports—for spectators and participants alike—are undoubtedly races. The tension mounts from the sound of the starter's gun right up to the last few yards, when the runners make a dash for the finish line, and you just can't help but get caught up in the excitement. And among the most popular races are those in which horse and rider are working together in elegant unison over the turf. Not too practical in the office, you may think, but then saddling up the office chair and galloping across the office carpet can be every bit as thrilling as if you were competing in the outdoor version.

YOU WILL NEED

- STRING
- MASKING TAPE
- SCISSORS
- COLORED PAPER
- CARDBOARD
- CHAIRS ON CASTERS

TIP *Much of the excitement of the racetrack is generated by betting. While this may not be in the spirit of your office Olympics, there's bound to be someone running a book on the finishing order, so it's probably best to bring this into the open and have an official bookmaker.*

The Track

First, create the track.

1 Plan a track around the office, and then clear it of all obstructions (it's best to stick to a flat race, since chairs are not too good at clearing jumps).

2 Appoint starters to hold a length of string across the starting line.

3 Mark out a finish line with masking tape.

WARNING *Because the riders are traveling at high speeds, identification can be difficult, so encourage the participants to wear distinctively colored outfits.*

The Runners and Riders

Now prepare the runners and riders.

1 Each competitor should cut out a horse-head shape from colored paper or cardboard to tape to the back of his or her chair.

2 Next, add long string reins to the horses' heads.

3 The competitors should now sit astride their reversed chairs.

4 They take the reins, and . . . they're off!

Office Free-running

Not one for the faint-hearted or the desk-bound, this: it really does take every ounce of stamina and courage. Free-running started out as a way of using the urban environment as an obstacle course for those unable to get out of the city for cross-country running, and is not usually thought of as an indoor activity, but elements of Parkour—as it is called—can be adapted for office use. Although free-running can be done simply for the hell of it, it's likely to arouse some curiosity among your coworkers, and they'll soon want to get involved, too. Make it a competitive sport by appointing judges to award points for technical merit, style, and so on, and deduct points for touching the floor, knocking over furniture, or refusing jumps. Some basic maneuvers are shown opposite.

WARNING

This activity requires extreme physical exertion and should not be attempted by anyone with health problems. If in doubt, seek professional advice. Care should always be taken to ensure that no damage is done to workplace property.

1| Leaping from file cabinet to file cabinet.

2| Swinging on doors.

TIP|*Before attempting the full circuit, practice the techniques needed (leaping, bouncing, hanging, swinging, and so on) until you are confident that you can tackle the obstacles without any major mishaps. Examine the course carefully in advance and plan a few exit strategies for those stages where you may find yourself stranded.*

3| Launching yourself onto a chair and then gliding to the next stage.

4| Traversing walls along radiators, air-conditioning units, and pipes.

5| Hanging from door frames.

continued on page 102

Office Free-running

Here's an example of a typical free-running office circuit, of moderate difficulty, showing many of the classic maneuvers. Every office is different, of course, and you'll soon be able to incorporate the quirks of your workplace into interesting challenges for the contestants.

TIP *No special equipment is needed, or even allowed, but sensible clothing is recommended; note that high-heeled shoes and pencil skirts are not the most practical garments to wear for free-running.*

WARNING *The cubicle-wall vault is spectacular, but it needs preparation: make sure that there is a suitable landing space (and an unoccupied cubicle) before launching yourself into that blind leap.*

1 Grip the top of the entrance door and swing 180°.

2 Flip onto the radiator and traverse the wall along the radiator, air-conditioning unit, and trash can, gripping the picture rail to steady yourself.

3 Leap up onto the top of the file cabinets.

4 Dive toward the bathroom door, grabbing the top of the door frame.

5 Hang from the door frame and then swing sideways onto the windowsill.

6 "Tightrope-walk" along the windowsill.

7 Fall backward into a sitting position on top of the water cooler and then twirl around to face the desk.

8 Vault over the cubicle wall (Fosbury flops are not recommended).

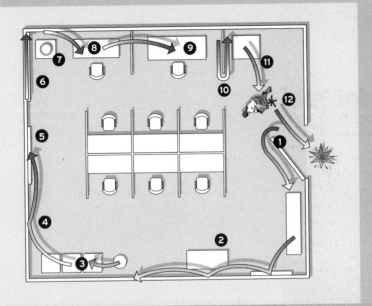

9 | Land on the desk in the next cubicle and then somersault to the next wall.

10 | Hanging by your fingertips, make your way around this wall and onto the final desk.

11 | From here, launch yourself onto a chair and land in a kneeling position as you grab the back of the chair.

12 | Glide smoothly and effortlessly to the finishing point.

TIP | *Design several courses of varying degrees of severity. This will encourage novices to give it a try, as well as letting the big boys of free-running show off to their hearts' content.*

WARNING | *Before hanging onto, or jumping onto, anything, make sure that it can take your weight. A good course designer should have ensured this, but don't take it for granted.*

Photocopier Steeplechase

One of the drawbacks of the chair derby (see pages 98–99) is that it can only be run on a flat surface, yet everyone enjoys a good jump. So, alas, you'll have to dispense with your steed for this race and instead get around the course on your own hind legs. Nevertheless, what it lacks in animal husbandry, photocopier steeplechase more than makes up for in thrills and spills. From the jostling for position at the starting line, through the falls and pile-ups at the jumps, right up to the final dash for the photocopier, this has to be one of the high points of any office Olympics.

Some suggestions to get you going . . .

This is essentially a race to be the first to reach the photocopier, despite the obstacles. Good course design is of the essence: not only the individual hurdles but also their placing (two or three in close succession, a high one just before or after a sharp bend in the course, and so on) can make the difference between a so-so and a go-go course.

Suggested Hurdles

TRASH-CAN WALL
Build this from overturned trash cans (what else?).

COMPUTER-CABLE FENCE
Construct this from cables (or string) tied from desk to desk across the course.

ROW OF CHAIRS
Runners have to jump up, onto the seat, then over the back of the chair.

WATER JUMP
A row of trash cans filled with water.

DITCH
Build two ramps out of reams of photocopier paper, with a long gap between them.

TIP | *An alternative is to make this more like show-jumping, with contestants running, one at a time, around the circuit against the clock. Penalties could be incurred for knocking over or refusing the jumps, and there could be a grand "jump off" to decide the outright winner.*

WARNING | *Keep a first-aid kit handy in case of falls. Do not call in a veterinarian, as they have a tendency to shoot any casualties.*

105

Workstation Tag

Kids' playground games are often fast and furious, but they can be quite cruel, too. Take the classic game of tag: everyone's a winner at the end of the game, except for the poor sap who was "it" last and was then treated like he had some contagious disease. More complex versions of the game have evolved (almost every playground has its own variations on the theme) to make it a more "winnable" sport, with rules being devised to suit the local conditions and terrain. Workstation tag is the latest in a long and noble line of such games.

VERSION 1

Draw straws (pencils) to decide who is "it" first. "It" chases and touches another player, who then becomes "it" until he or she can touch someone else. This can go on indefinitely.

VERSION 2

From the moment that "it" leaves her workstation, anybody that she touches has to freeze on the spot, or else go to a designated holding area. This continues until all of the players have been tagged or an agreed time limit has been reached.

VERSION 3

Players are divided into two teams and play as in version 2, touching members of the opposing team. They can also free their teammates from frozen or captive suspension from the game by touching them, leading to some interesting counterrelease tactics.

WARNING | *A good game of workstation tag can be spread out over several days and could make its way out of the office into the hall, cafeteria, or even the parking lot during lunch and coffee breaks. Make it a rule that anywhere outside the company premises is a "safe" area, to avoid any accusations of stalking.*

OPTIONAL ADDITIONAL RULES

1 | Certain areas of the office can be designated "home base" (around the water cooler or coffee machine, for example) and are then "safe" zones where you cannot be tagged.

2 | Players may not spend more than five minutes in "home base" zones.

3 | Hiding in closets, under desks, or in bathrooms is restricted to five minutes only.

4 | An umpire should be appointed to arbitrate on disputed touches where there are no independent witnesses.

File-cabinet Climbing

Some sports are more about pitting humankind against nature than winning or losing, and the ultimate challenge for most people is mountaineering. Unless you like the idea of clambering out of the office window, however, there isn't that much to climb in the average workplace. But then, if the whole building were tilted 90° (OK, that's a bit of a leap of the imagination), the floor would make a pretty good cliff face, and there's a range of office furniture just crying out to be conquered, culminating in the peak of the big file cabinet. But why would you want to get to the top of the file cabinet anyway? Because it's there . . .

1 | Rope the members of the team together with string attached to belt buckles, suspenders, bra straps, whatever. Establish base camp (the water cooler is as good a place as any).

2 Traverse the floor. This takes a little imagination: the horizontal is now your vertical, so you'll be tackling this either prostrate or on all fours.

3 When you get to the first overhang (probably a desk), climb over it, securing your ropes to a computer, telephone, or a similar mainstay. Make your teammates aware of any outstanding handholds or footholds, and tie ropes around any sheer faces where there is nothing to hold onto. Continue to the file cabinet.

4 Once you reach the peak of the file cabinet, fly your flag (perhaps bearing the company logo), relax, and enjoy the view.

TIP | *Not much harm can come to you if there is a mishap on the file-cabinet face, but that doesn't mean that you shouldn't take sensible precautions. Making your way across the floor may look safe enough, but carpet burns can be a problem, and some office furniture can have horribly sharp edges, so beware.*

Water-cooler Flash Mobbing

Another noncompetitive game to play for the sheer hell of it—and to bewilder, annoy, and generally rattle anybody not in on the secret—is water-cooler flash mobbing. It's all pretty pointless, really, but enormous fun, and it does help to bring people together. It's simplicity itself to organize: you just specify a time and place where everyone should congregate and for how long, and then watch it happen. There's something eerie about the entire office workforce homing in on one place, reminiscent of TV wildlife documentaries about swarms and herds, as well as those 1950s zombie and body-snatcher movies. On the other hand, it can also lead to some great office parties.

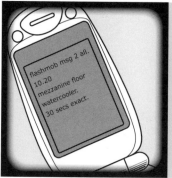

flashmob msg 2 all.
10.20
mezzanine floor
watercooler.
30 secs exact.

1 Send a text message to a colleague via your cell phone, or else e-mail him or her, giving details of the proposed flash mob (having allowed enough time for the message to be disseminated around the office).

2| You could also specify some other instructions: wear a hat, walk very slowly, or hold a large letter W in front of your face . . .

3| Your colleague should then text or e-mail two of his or her colleagues in the same way, thus setting the chain in motion. In no time at all, the message will be passed around a sizable proportion of the workforce.

4| At the appointed time, a crowd will form at the specified place and will then magically disperse. Spooky.

TIP| *It's absolutely essential to keep quiet about the proposed flash mob before, after, and during the event. It should appear mysteriously spontaneous to any outsiders, or the effect will be lost. The period just afterward, when everything suddenly returns to normal, is particularly important: onlookers (particularly bosses) often can't believe what just happened.*

Office Regatta

An English varsity favorite for hundreds of years, rowing has recently become a popular sport since its inclusion in the Olympics. And now, thanks to the technological marvel that is the modern caster, you don't have to be an Ivy League type, or even have access to a suitable river, in order to participate in it yourself. Just line up some well-oiled office chairs, take your seats, and push off down the hallway. Old hands at this can pass on their valuable experience by acting as trainers, shouting advice through bullhorns as they follow the teams on their bicycles.

TIP | *Traditionally, rowing teams are known as "eights," for self-explanatory reasons. Unfortunate experience has shown that such a large team is impractical in all but the largest of offices, and that a team of five would seem to be the norm. Some office rowers may want to go solo, but this doesn't have the spectator appeal of the team event.*

1 | Clear a path through the middle of the office or a hallway that is wide enough for the rowers to move down without running aground on either side.

2 | Form teams of five (with an additional trainer for each team if necessary). The four rowers should sit on office chairs, one behind the other, with their backs facing the direction of the course; the coxswain should sit on her office chair facing them.

3 | At the signal from the coxswain, the rowers should pull imaginary oars, and then push back with both feet on the ground, propelling them along the course. The coxswain should set the pace and ensure that the strokes are being made in unison.

4 | The trainer should follow on his bicycle (if used), shouting encouragement and instructions through his bullhorn.

5

EXTREME OFFICE

Thus far, the pastimes in this book have come into the category of "harmless fun"; the only person that you're likely to hurt is yourself (and then you're only likely to sustain a bruise on the butt, a sprained ankle, or a staple in the thumb), and the greatest danger that they pose is getting caught by the office supervisor. And even if you are found doing them on office time, it's likely that you'll get away with just a reprimand. For most of us, that's as far as we want to go.

But for some, the daredevils among the workforce, it's not the game that attracts, but the risk factor. Unless the stakes are high, these madcaps find even the most exciting sports too tame. Always on the lookout for an even more perilous thrill, they're the sorts who spend their vacations skyboarding, trekking across Antarctica, or wrestling grizzly bears.

So, for you intrepid souls who want to know more, we have taken the subtitle of this book—*50 Things to Do in the Office That Won't Get You a Pink Slip*—with a grain of salt and have upped the ante: these are the extreme office pastimes. While you may not risk life and limb by trying any of them, you do run the risk of making powerful enemies, and even of putting your job on the line. Read on, if you dare . . .

Online In-house Blog

- A COMPUTER
- INFORMATION TECHNOLOGY (IT) DEPARTMENT SUPPORT

Office gossip is a well-established way of spreading misinformation around a company. The grapevine extends throughout the whole building, and sometimes beyond, ensuring that no confidences remain secret for more than a couple days at most. Once again, this process can be improved by using the latest technology: the Internet is an ideal medium for disseminating information quickly, and the blog is the perfect way to set tongues wagging and eyebrows raising. Reading rumors on a computer screen not only gives them the oxygen of publicity but also an air of authority.

WARNING *Being the font of all office knowledge is a great feeling, but be careful! Above all, preserve your anonymity. It's horribly easy to give yourself away with careless talk or bragging, but you can trust absolutely nobody. And remember, you've probably offended, embarrassed, defamed, and enraged some people in high places.*

1| If you don't work in the IT department and have limited computer skills, befriend a similarly subversive nerd to help.

2| Set up a blog that cannot be traced back to you, or even your department. Give yourself, and your blog, a suitably cryptic name, such as deepthroat@watercoolergate or fink@officewhispers.

3| Pick up as much gossip from around the office as you can, and then dish the dirt via your blog. If you can't find any juicy tidbits, invent some. Encourage readers to contribute tittle-tattle.

4| Publicize your blog by telling colleagues that you have stumbled across something that they really shouldn't miss. The whole thing will snowball in no time.

Pod Wars

If you're in one of those offices that have abandoned high-walled cubicles in favor of those more open-plan clusters of desks known as pods, you're probably working for a company that is keen to encourage team spirit. Never mind that you just want to be left alone to do your job, hobby, time-wasting, or whatever, you must remember that "there isn't an 'I' in team." Instead of grumbling, why not take this to its logical extreme and be territorial? Why not stir up a bit of patriotism in your pod, put up some defenses, and invade a few rivals?

YOU WILL NEED

- OFFICE FURNITURE
  (for building fortifications)
- RULERS
- RUBBER BANDS
- SMALL PAPER PELLETS
- CORRECTION FLUID
- PAPER CLIPS

WARNING | *It may all start out fairly harmlessly, but conflicts have a habit of escalating. Skirmishes can lead to battles, the breakdown of diplomatic relations, and eventually all-out war, which can be counterproductive in the workplace. Hostilities and loyalties run deep, too, and even in peacetime can lead to a pod cold war.*

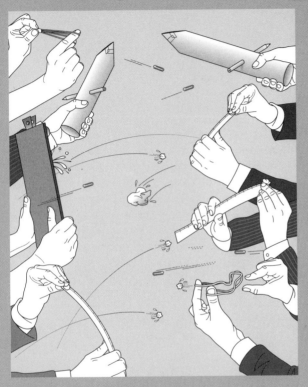

➲ Send warning salvos of wadded-up paper shells and paper clips catapulted across with rubber bands or flicked with rulers.

➲ Form alliances with neighboring pods to counter any threatening superpods.

➲ Develop a weapon of mass destruction as a deterrent: perhaps germ warfare (a selective computer virus), a biological weapon (something unpleasant in the coffee machine), or an explosive . . . hey, I'm not going to give all my military secrets away.

➲ Fortify your pod. Build a defensive wall out of office furniture, trash cans, and other office objects.

➲ Get together with your podmates and hash out a defense strategy—preemptive retaliation is always a winner.

➲ Organize forays into enemy territory to commandeer scarce resources (paper clips, tape, coffee cups, and so on) or to cut off vital supplies (get between your enemies and the water cooler, for instance, or switch off their electricity at the wall).

121

Boss Baiting

YOU WILL NEED

- A GOOD TEAM SPIRIT
- CARDBOARD, PENCILS, AND FELT-TIP MARKERS
- ELASTIC THREAD
- (SEE POD WARS, PAGES 120–121)

The American Society for the Prevention of Cruelty to Animals (ASPCA) has, quite rightly, put an end to the horrific cruelty of such so-called sports as bear baiting and bullfighting, and even alligator wrestling is under review. No longer are petty criminals punished by public humiliation in the stocks, either. While we must applaud this action on humanitarian grounds, it has left a bit of a hole in the market for assuaging the nastier side of our natures—who is there left for us to vent our pent-up aggression and frustration on? Yeah, right: the boss. I mean, he's not exactly a cuddly animal, is he? Or even human . . .

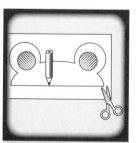

1 | Draw a pair of bear ears on a piece of cardboard. Add details and color with pencils and markers. Cut out.

2 | Make a hole on either side using a hole punch. Thread elastic through and secure by knotting.

Some suggestions to get you going . . .

Everyone in the office should take turns annoying the boss in some petty way, until he finally loses it.

DRAW LOTS

Do this to establish in what order people should needle the boss.

IRRITANTS

Assign a different irritant to each person. These should depend on the victim's personal foibles but could include: serving his coffee cold, spilling the same, delivering documents in random order, doing everything just a few minutes late, backing out of his office bowing . . . you'll know what really sets him off.

THE WINNER

The winner is the person whose annoyance is the final straw for your boss.

THE TROPHY

Award trophy "ears of the bear" made of cardboard.

TIP | *This is a really risky one. If the boss calls your bluff, pass the buck whenever possible and blame some other poor sap, or, failing that, explain your way out of it by telling him that it's all part of an office initiative-building course.*

TIP | *If you're too chicken to take any risks yourself, or are simply a power-freak, engineer things so that everyone else does the baiting at your bidding.*

Parking-lot Ticktacktoe

Board games: you either love 'em or you hate 'em (and I'm not talking about what the directors of the firm get up to in their weekly meetings). Even chess, the pinnacle of intellectual pursuits for some, leaves others cold. Unless, that is, it's one of those outdoor games with outsize pieces, or, better still, a game in which humans stand in for the pieces. Then it becomes a spectacle and attracts crowds of interested onlookers. You may think that the simple—even puerile—game of ticktacktoe was an unlikely candidate for the spectator-sport treatment, but you'd be surprised . . .

1| Overnight, rope off an area of the staff parking lot and make it look as though it is about to be resurfaced or reserved for visiting dignitaries. Put up a notice to that effect. Make sure that it is big enough to accommodate the game (a square of 3 x 3 spaces is required) and, ideally, that it is visible from your department to enable spectator encouragement.

2 | Divide your colleagues into two teams of similar-colored-automobile owners (the automobiles, not the owners), for example, five red and five green.

3 | Toss a coin to decide who goes first.

4 | Take turns making excuses to leave the office, and then sneak out and move an automobile into the grid.

5 | The rules are the same as those for regular ticktacktoe, and the first team to form a line of three automobiles is the winner.

Correction Fluid-Balling

Those awful middle-management initiative-training weekends—you know the kind of thing, where they teach you survival techniques in the middle of nowhere and drill you like it's a boot camp—usually include at least one session of paintballing (which, I have to admit, can be quite fun). Some people have developed a taste for this, and even pay to do it on their own time, but there's really no need to go to all that trouble. Now that we're all computerized, there's gallons of correction fluid in the supply closet, and any schoolboy can tell you how to make weapons out of the contents of your desk.

The ammo . . .

Make pellets from small wads of paper dipped into correction fluid. These must be fired before they dry, so get a production line going. Load blow pipes with rolled-up paper tubes.

The weapons . . .

Here are some ideas for the weapons that you could make.

TIP | *A business suit is probably the best camouflage in an office setting, since real camouflage is a bit, well, conspicuous, especially if it includes foliage. All the same, you may not want to wear your usual work clothes in view of the mess involved, so perhaps you should confine your correction fluid-balling to casual days.*

1| Make a crossbow by taping a pencil to a ruler and looping around a strong rubber band.

2| A rubber-band catapult.

3| A ruler ballista.

4| A pen blow pipe.

Undercover Business

Go on, admit it: you've always liked the idea of being a double agent working undercover like in those spy movies, haven't you? It's nothing to be ashamed of, everybody thinks that—but only the daring few actually put it into practice. You probably don't work for a company that has some secret ingredient that you can sell to a competitor (who wants to know how you make your second-rate products anyway?), so the alternative is obvious: set up your own rival business empire from within. You'll enjoy all of the excitement of devising clandestine machinations, and it can be quite lucrative, too.

Some suggestions to get you going . . .

Keep your idea simple yet brilliant. Do your research thoroughly and aim to fulfill a service, a need, or a desire that your colleagues just can't live without. The advice on the opposite page will help.

WARNING | *We cannot condone the appropriation and sale of company property for personal gain, and we deplore disloyalty among employees. This game is intended as a fantasy entertainment played for favors or tokens, not as a business venture for monetary profit.*

THE BUSINESS

Decide what it is you're going to sell. This could be hardware, such as office stationery or rejects from the production line; or software, such as information, client lists, and so on.

ESTABLISH A CUSTOMER BASE

Call around to test the water. What you're looking for are clients who are unscrupulous, or desperate, enough to want to pay for what you're selling. Word will soon get around, so be careful whom you approach.

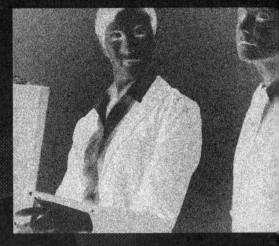

CORNER THE MARKET

If you can control, for example, the entire supply of soap, paper hand towels, toilet rolls, and similar essential items for the company bathrooms, you've guaranteed yourself a nice, steady income.

THIS IS THE REALLY RISKY BIT

If your venture takes off as you hope, you'll have to recruit others. Who can you trust to join you without blowing your operation out of the water? And is it possible that they would double-cross you and set up their own firm?

GETTING PAID

Payment into a numbered Swiss bank account is unrealistic. Internal customers can reimburse you with favors (taking your shift, for example, or bringing you your daily coffee and pastry), but external contacts must pay on a strictly cash basis.

WARNING Resist the temptation to dress the part. Wearing a Bond-style tux or a ratty raincoat will sort of give the game away.

Office-chair Downhill Skiing

For the real speed freaks, most of the activities you can do in the office might seem a little, er, pedestrian. Not so this one, which captures all the thrill and danger of downhill skiing in miniature. Of course, it takes a bit of reorganization of the office furniture to give you a good long run, but it's also an excellent spectator sport, so nobody will mind—just line up your colleagues on either side of the piste to shout encouragement.

WARNING | *It's vitally important that the slope is fixed securely to the desk (and the ski jump firmly anchored to the floor). Ordinary sticky tape just isn't man enough for the job, so use heavy-duty duct tape if you can get it. Inviting the janitor to participate should guarantee a supply of the equipment you need.*

1| Make a slope by dismantling the dividing screen between two cubicles and leaning this against a desk. Tape this securely in place. Clear the desk, and put an office chair on it.

2| Clear the area at the bottom of the slope of all obstructions.

Optional extras

At the bottom of the piste, mark out a slalom using trash cans (*see step 3*). Make a smaller ramp at the bottom of the downhill section to form a ski jump by using a bulletin board propped up on boxes of stationery (*see step 2*).

WARNING| *You'd be amazed how fast you can go on an office chair (well, more terrified than amazed) and how much damage you can do to office furniture, innocent bystanders, and yourself. You have been warned.*

TIP| *You could also organize some après ski around the coffee machine for when you've reached the bottom of the slopes.*

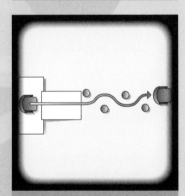

3| Sit on the chair. Now use a couple of brooms from the broom closet for ski poles, push off, and whiz down the slope and across the floor.

Creative Lighting

YOU WILL NEED

- IT SKILLS
- ACCESS TO THE STAFF DATABASE AND OFFICE LIGHT SWITCHES
- A COOPERATIVE JANITOR AND SECURITY STAFF

It's not a new idea, but creative illumination of the office building is still very effective, and planning a grid can take up hours of otherwise dead time. The taller and more extreme office buildings become, the more fun it is, too. You'll need reasonable IT skills to figure out which lights will go on and off where (think of them as giant pixels on a grid). The choice of slogan or message can be tricky: rude words are funny but may get you a pink slip (although if you already have one of those, they can spell sweet revenge). Go for short, simple sports or seasonal themes, or the company's mission statement in a nutshell. Symbols and icons will work as well as words. Don't forget to photograph your better efforts.

1| Spell out your message or slogan using a grid of the building's windows re-created on your computer. Keep it simple to start with.

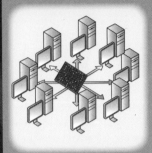

2 When you have completed the grid, merge it with the mailing list and let everyone know whether they should switch their lights on or off.

3 At this point, the plan depends on the goodwill and enthusiasm of your colleagues. Encourage cooperation by allowing them to choose their own slogans.

4 Go outside to check that the slogan appears as you planned. Organize building "conversations" with colleagues in other office megabuildings.

TIP *Check that all lights are working before the final display. Persuade a famous celebrity (or maybe the janitor) to announce the great switch on.*

133

Fax-paper Gladiator

Remember the fax machine? Oh, come on, it wasn't that long ago. An indispensable addition to every office, capable of sending copies of documents instantly (well, sort of, and I guess that the quality wasn't exactly perfect), until, like Betamax videos, cassette players, and the typewriter, it was superseded. So what happened to all of the rolls of that shiny, thermal paper? Take a look in the back of the supply closet, and I guarantee that you'll find stacks of it. Fax-paper rolls are totally useless now, except for one thing: gladiator games. With a little preparation, they'll provide the weapon that you need to become a second Russell Crowe.

Some suggestions to get you going . . .

Any noncombatants can form a mob baying for blood, and one could be chosen to be the Roman emperor or empress. He or she should then make the life-or-death decision when a disarmed gladiator is cornered or floored: the thumbs-up or thumbs-down sign will determine his fate.

1 Rolls of fax paper can be telescoped outward and taped in place to make spears.

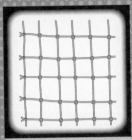

2 Knot string to make a net large enough to throw over your opponent's head. Use it in conjunction with a spear or trident.

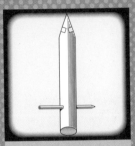

3 Mailing tubes purloined from the mail room, flattened and sharpened at one end, make short swords.

4 Clipboards are ideal as bucklers (little shields), while laptop cases make bigger shields (for wimps), to be used with the swords.

5 Costumes are not strictly necessary but add to the fun. Men should strip to the waist and wear a short skirt (make this out of sheets of cardboard tucked into your belt) and sandals; the women in Roman arenas generally just wore long robes and got thrown to the lions.

TIP *It's fun to think up Latin names for yourselves. How about Gluteus Maximus or Sportacus Officius?*

Office Dares

A lot of good games involve an element of chance as well as risk: betting on the roll of the dice or the dealing of cards, for example. Updating the unpredictability of the kids' game of "spin the bottle," and adapting the dares to suit an office environment, gives you a high-risk pursuit that's sure to get the epinephrine pumping. Players' hearts will be in their throats as they stake their office credibility on the spin of a cell phone, and reputations—even jobs—have been lost to the addictive lure of office dares. Of course, as the initiator of the game, you'll get to set the rules as "daremaster," at least until the end of the first season.

Some suggestions to get you going . . .

Award points for dare-fulfillment, or impose penalties (deduct points from someone's score, for instance) for the nonfulfillment of dares. Enter the points on a scoreboard, and, at the end of the month, see who has accumulated the most. The winner gets to be the daremaster for the next month and is exempt from participating while he or she runs the competition and decides on the list of dares.

YOU WILL NEED

- CARDBOARD
- A FELT-TIP MARKER
- GLUE
- THUMBTACKS
- A BALLPOINT PEN
- A CELL PHONE
- A THICK SKIN

136

Wheel of fortune

Make a wheel of fortune on cardboard with a ballpoint pointer, as follows.

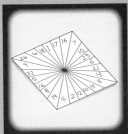

1| On a square piece of cardboard, draw radiating lines from the center to divide it into, perhaps, twenty-four segments; write a different number in each segment at random.

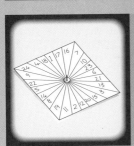

2| Glue a thumbtack, pointed up, to the center of the card.

3| Skewer a ballpoint pen (some of them have a hole in the side for precisely this purpose) on the thumbtack so that it balances and spins freely without spinning off.

Wheel of time

Make a wheel of time as follows.

1| Make a similar wheel but divide the card into eight segments and write time limitations in each of these.

2| Spin the cell phone. Whoever it points to has to spin the wheel of fortune and accept the dare.

3| See which number the pointer landed on and look it up on the list of dares (see pages 138-139).

4| Spin the wheel of time to see how long your victim has to carry out the dare, and then tell him or her to get out there and do it.

TIP| *Make the cell-phone spinning a daily, or even twice-daily, event, maybe doing it every coffee break.*

continued on page 138

Office Dares

The daremaster is in sole charge of the list of dares. Once a player has spun the wheel of fortune, the daremaster consults the list and informs the poor soul, in secret, what he or she will have to do. This list is a confidential document, and its contents should not be divulged to anyone until the dare is completed, except in cases of dispute.

TIP | *To discourage people from chickening out, deduct double the number of points if they fail to achieve a particular dare. At the end of the competition, anybody with minus points should suffer the contempt of the rest of the department, be treated as a pariah, and be forced to do all of the menial tasks around the office.*

SUGGESTIONS

Here is a list of twenty-four dares and their points; note that they are merely suggestions intended to give you an idea of the sorts of things that you can get people to do.

ONE-POINT DARES

1 | Walk backward into, and out of, a meeting.

2 | Leave your shoes outside the office door with a note saying "For cleaning."

3 | Wear rubber gloves all day; answer all inquiries with "You don't want to know."

4 | When walking down a hallway, or the stairs, trip and stumble at every fifth step.

5 | After your first sip of coffee, rush from the room, clutching your stomach.

6 | Spend half an hour in a bathroom stall, groaning audibly.

THREE-POINT DARES

7 | Phone the IT Department repeatedly, telling them that you think that you've caught a virus from your computer.

8 | Pick up somebody's coffee-time cookie or snack, examine it carefully, and then put it back, shaking your head.

9 | Answer your phone with "Sam's Chinese laundry, how may I help you?" delivered in a French or Italian accent.

10 | Challenge all friendly greetings with "What's it to you?"

11 | Every half-hour, shout "Avalanche!" and run out of the office.

12 | Stand in the elevator and shake hands with whoever comes in, welcoming them to your humble abode.

FIVE-POINT DARES

13 | Tell your office supervisor that you need Friday off because you're going to have a headache.

14 | Leave a signed Valentine card on a colleague's desk (no matter what time of year it is).

15 | Send a blanket e-mail to everyone in your entire address book, asking if anyone will accompany you to your first Sex Addicts Anonymous meeting.

16 | Inform your manager that, under the provisions of Article 9 of the Contagious Diseases Act, it would be unwise to meet with him.

17 | Leave your zipper (or blouse) open all morning, and if anyone points it out, say "The heat, man, the heat!"

18 | Lie on your back, under the spout of the water cooler, gasping "Water, water, I must have water."

TEN-POINT DARES

19 | Inform your boss that you've composed a company anthem, then go into her office and sing it to her.

20 | When asked your opinion in a meeting, reply "Don't know, don't care," and fold your arms.

21 | Go down on one knee, head bowed, when talking to a superior.

22 | Use the sales meeting as an opportunity to do a little drug dealing.

23 | Provide spurious evidence to your boss that the firm's been infiltrated by terrorists, the CIA, or aliens.

24 | Wink at your boss, tap the side of your nose, and say "Your secret's safe with me."

Water-cooler Whispers

This is a version of telephone, a dull game played by passing a whispered message on, and seeing how distorted it has become when the last person says it out loud. The water cooler is the hub of the office rumor mill anyway, so adapt the game to suit local conditions. Start a rumor, any rumor. Whisper it to just one colleague and then swear him or her to secrecy. Back at your workstation, note down the date and time, and then see how long it takes until the distorted rumor is fed back to you.

1 Person A whispers something innocuous to person B, for example, "I hear that John from the mail room is getting a new chair."

TIP *Here's how to make the rumor mill grind even faster:*
➲ *take your cell phone to the water cooler to spread a wider net*
➲ *e-mail everybody as news comes in*
➲ *deny everything—this will fan the flames*

2| At the next water-cooler moment, person B tells persons C and D that John is in line for a new chair.

3| Persons C and D meet persons E, F, and G and tell them that they have heard for sure that the new chair is for John.

4| Everybody clusters around the water cooler to badmouth John's meteoric, and totally undeserved, rise to stardom.

5| Person G tells person A that mailroom John has been appointed chairman of the board. It has taken twelve minutes.

Index

Acknowledgments

The publishers would like to thank
the following for permission to
reproduce their pictures:

p. 111 © White Packert/Iconica/
Getty Images; pp. 24, 46, and 47
(background) © istockphoto.